Sur barely contains itself. David Kc collection with the thick sounds of hard syllables striking the earth, shaking it. I love the density of these poems, the depth of observation—so much here that rewards multiple readings. Koehn is inclusive yet precise in his noticing. He embraces incompletion and mystery, while also giving them room to breathe. These poems turn on their surprising intimacies. There are no consolation prizes to be had here, but sometimes there is consolation. And even, sometimes, love.

—Jim Daniels, author of *Digger's Blues*

Animated by "the invention of song, people in pain," David Koehn's *Sur* ventures us into meadows, deltas, all kinds of traffic and tax returns. Beloveds and creatures abound here. And wild grasses. A feast of peaty, alluvial soils. These irreverent poems interrogate the biggest ideas and the smallest. How do we love and injure? How do we "shape the shore of the world from the boat"? How do we behold a spider web across a trail after a night of rain? Language meanders, dizzyingly, intelligently, and thinks. What complicity, what grief, what water? And when we put these mutinous poems down again, there they appear, in full relief: our harmful ways. Our gentle hands.

—Nathalie Khankan, author of *Quiet Orient Riot*

David Koehn's *Sur* seamlessly plays sound and form with and against the speaker's perception of the natural world. The poems rejoice in the landscape's negative space, positing, "What do we call the empty space between winter's branches?" Koehn's mystical speaker is constantly questing to name and not name liminal spaces, asking, "Can the morning hold only one idea,/ Does uncertainty feel only one way?" Throughout these agile poems that deftly embody lists, incantations, and lyrical fragments, each engages the act of seeing as a sense of revelation and shape-shifting until the speaker prophesizes, "You have become a thing concealed. A part of the kaleidoscope." Sure enough, you, the reader, will merge with the wild colors and revel in the refracted pastoral, the disrupted elegy, and the striking turns until, much like the narrator, "My body/ Is your body, I want to hurt you,/ I want to hurt myself."

—Maria Nazos, author of *PULSE*

Previously Published Works

Poetry

Coil
(University of Alaska / Permafrost, 1998, 2006)
winner of the Midnight Sun Chapbook Contest

Tunic
(speCt books, 2013)

Twine
(Bauhan Publishing, 2014)
winner of the May Sarton New Hampshire Poetry Prize

Scatterplot
(Omnidawn, 2020)

Criticism edited by David Koehn

Compendium: A Collection of Thoughts on Prosody by Donald Justice

SUR

Cover art and cover design by Jeffrey Pethybridge

Cover typeface:
Interior typeface: Athelas and Didot
Interior design by Laura Joakimson

Library of Congress Cataloging-in-Publication Data

Names: Koehn, David, author.
Title: Sur / by David Koehn.
Other titles: Sur (Compilation)
Description: Oakland : Omnidawn Publishing, 2024. | Summary: "Poetry that
explores wildness and composes a landscape of complex human emotions.
Drawing on a range of stylistic influences, the poetry of Sur takes on
the essence of connection and the ways in which we continually develop
meaning about others and to the natural world. With this collection,
David Koehn paints a landscape where wilderness intertwines with human
emotions and grows between ill-fitting interpersonal connections. Sur
invites readers to step back and look critically at their world while
remaining intimately intertwined with it. Throughout, imagery of
nature-like a snake drinking from a stream, or a mountain god-blends
with the emotional landscape of tumultuous relationships, exploring
themes of wildness and an inevitable unraveling of secrets."-- Provided
by publisher.

Identifiers: LCCN 2024035257 | ISBN 9781632431585 (trade paperback)
Subjects: BISAC: POETRY / General | LCGFT: Poetry.
Classification: LCC PS3611.O3626 S87 2024 | DDC 811/.6--dc23/eng/20240816
LC record available at https://lccn.loc.gov/2024035257

Published by Omnidawn Publishing, Oakland, California
www.omnidawn.com
10 9 8 7 6 5 4 3 2 1
ISBN: 978-1-63243-158-5

S U R

David Koehn

Omnidawn Publishing
Oakland, California
2024

light quickening
on the ocean expanse
like
a skirmish of knives

Neruda, "Ode to Light on the Sea"

Contents

Inhale

The dusty cider jugs, through the windows
Of the green door aside the embarrassingly red
Flowers of the ivy geranium, wait to be filled.

The corrugated tin of the awning channels
Water away from the leaky woodwork around
A rectangular picture window. The lemon

Tree presides over the chicken coop from inside
The wired pen. How do we love the decomposing
Pumpkin? Pockmarked, receding into its unresisting

Flesh, come close to me. Lay your head on my chest.

Working Backwards

This collage will air dry just after a shellacking
Of wheat paste coats the strips of music,
The arcs of empty crossword puzzles,
The geometries of partly cloudy skies.
All emerge through window frame cut from the B
In the window's E of the house. The H-shape
Of chair snipped from the chair. Linda's call cuts

The music in the air from its mobile,
A suspension of sailboats tacking the ennui
Of worry into a distant journey's tilted
Keel. Dried violets muddied in the glue:
She describes a TV Show where a philandering
Husband gets his comeuppance. This is the map.
A latitude and longitude of this stravaig clipped
Into one-inch squares and pasted into every third pane.

You make your bed the garden box of coincidences.
One year the year of concord grapes, another the year
Of radishes and zucchini, the next, one box
Always a plenty, the untended, irrepressible
Suite of edible not-quite-lovelies: tumbleweed,
Goosefoot, common yarrow, mingled
With the untamed delicacies: borage,
Nasturtiums, rosemary, and the cosmos.

Halving

Someone is playing the piano, someone is listening,
And the pampas grass and its willingness
Redirect the wind. Is there a more perverse flower
Then the waterfall trumpet of a tobacco plant, ½ itself
Then halved more or less again, halving the space
As it fills with the scent, coincidentally, of a match
Blown out. Someone's head angles into the delight.

Last night's burr between smorzando cliffs
Has been replaced by the promise of moonglade.
The wish: that each of you do exactly as you wish.

A grill has replaced last night's swordfish
Tidily sown like hard corals in an atoll. Bone-in

Chicken thighs squabble with the grilled garlic.

After Taking a Picture of "The Water Atlas" at the Big Break Guest Center (Delta 27)

Who has half a mind? Please shop the local
Used clothing store to buy six green cardigans.
The nail gun pops trim. Her life?
One long Oulipo exercise
Never using "it." Bay says, "Maybe he's a predator.
Maybe he eats pollinators." We go nowhere together,
A scroll describes how we walk here.
12 hours ago, Anthony Bourdain hung
Himself in a hotel room in Paris.
This is not the first time death has dragged a noose
Around the house. Family. Friends. Friends of friends.
A catfish flops about in the canvas hammock of a folding chair.
A kayak wobbles.
A teenage boy drops a backpack off his back.
The relief map of the delta
Navigates the eye from Frank's Tract to Rio Vista.
Along the trail, the bucket
Of a clam-shell dredge has passed out face first
Between the pond and the field grass.
While Muir battled the Hetch Hetchy dam,
The scooped delta, the manufactured islands
Grabbed farmland for the disappointed.
Menopause drifts through the reeds.
Quince, fig, peacock, pomegranate, a pierced cornea
Changes the world. Underneath our feet
The bass line of Wordsworth,
"Come forth into the light of things." Fuck your helplessness.
When your lover asks you to slap them, slap them twice
And see where you stand. We have all been manufactured

And lack blind spot detection. Outside,
The stems of a scrawny 100-year-old Sequoia.
Nat holds a ½" Wood Carving
Fish Tail No. 54, the sweep nicks the edge
Of an edge to give an S a serif finish.
One knows the right amount of ink
By the kissing sound as the block lifts.
Consider Mel Brooks' *History of the World Part 1*,
After the cave painting, the invention
Of the expert, the cave painting pissed on.
The invention of song, people
In pain; the past agrees.
Morning Glories greet the door to the house,
Inside a mouth the mongering mantis
Hopes for the hassle. In the back of an electrician's van,
Wiring for a room of a friend of your brother-in-law.
Both afraid to wipe their face in the pink towel
Hanging in the shared wash closet
At the end of the hall in the northeast of Paris,
Reyna sees Lulu for the first time.
And the Private Property sign
Knit into the grey cotton t-shirt
Left on the side of the road near the creek
Where Bay and I measure the river otter's
Return by the freshness of the stool
And the river oyster shell mosaic,
Someone in a sweatshirt pockets
The text of the front matter.
"...for going out, I found, was really going in..."
Is what Muir said. The 8' effluent pipe next to us,
A straw aside a long lost
Mixed drink. Is that right?
The quilted canvas cotton headboard

Contrasted to a bag of hard candy
Scattered over the newspaper. Letter
X sent my doppelganger a scarf made
Of woven Spanish moss.
If you texted her would she reply?
Would she stop her Yoga class, the Brooklyn
Traffic arguing in the auroratone, and reply?
She would say, "you should have."
If you were never encouraged to join
How would you interpret that?
I grew up thinking we holiday everywhere together.
In Mudcrutch's "Trailer," listen to Petty's drag
"I had to go for a mobile home."
But when all is forgotten there will always be
The lagging indicator—
The aroma of Vesuvio's pizza parlor,
The yeasty sweatiness of linoleum-soaked
In decades of freshly baked pizza
—like a door opening
To a room full of treasure long forgotten
Like an unexpected tax return refund.
No work of art is any better than a wax museum:
Every avatar takes the place
Of another avatar. My daughter, Anna,
Is a hummingbird, my son, Bay, a flycatcher.
A shard of the broken mirror
In the dirt reflects the face of a stranger.
An eye traces the clear glassy surface of the water.
The coffee cup empty of coffee reminds the green
Light there is no innermost self.
What water? What delta in what change of your mind?
To shape the shore of the world from the boat.

The Black Lagoon

It's a sci-fi myth.
A star 24
Wooden windmill rests
Atop a handmade
Tower, its neuron
Pattern of laughter
After a joke told
Well, in the largesse
Of a cottonwood,
Brobdingnagian,
Its crooks loom over
The local orchard
The well-lit Little
League field occupied
By the night game, ignores
The steel stanchions
And their alien
Illuminations:
Garlic, corn, cherry
Tree, strawberry fields,
Red helicopters.
Every slough guards
The Himalayan
Blackberry's cradle.
Passage of olive
Branches, abandoned
Cup of coffee, grain
Elevators ship
Anticipated
Cargo lovers slick
With each other roll

In the mud, we Sunday
The remembered film
Of a matinee
With Julie Adams,
*Creature from the Black
Lagoon*—desperate
For love, we kill ourselves.

Vanguard

The limping wooden picnic table at the edge of the ocean's cliffside
feeds the conversation
Between two ravens. I rub the scent of pine off my pointer and thumb on
your back and thighs.
I have this idea of myself as Anna's hummingbird, red-necklaced,
needling the firecracker
Plant, considering the purple head of the flowering chives, considering
and dismissing
The leadwort. The fraught, dizzying hum of the frenetic obsessions
suddenly paused
For considerations of danger from the chimeric beetle alighting and the
recognition:
Patience is the vanguard of love. It is, of course, all a joke. I am the
common geranium
Or an idea of it that dove eggs with delight, rashly signaling like the trail
ahead,
"See me. Inhale my hints of lemon and ginger. Come to me. Come with
me. Consume me."

14

exact

glances

                              break

            us

A Spider Web Across the Pine Ridge Trail the Morning After a Night of Rain (Delta 23)

Attaches everything, strand to stump,
Another to neighboring limb, another
To bent stalk of corn, another to empty
Beer bottle and rock underneath.
On silk, drops of water refract
Bay's eye looking in from the other side.
Collect and disperse the fogginess
Clinging to the earth as the sun gets in gear.
Almost nothing has started humming yet.
Can the morning hold only one idea,
Does uncertainty feel only one way?
The idea of now is just a cover tune.
See "This Must Be The Place" by Sure Sure
And wait for the organ solo. Now's PR rep
Keeps insisting on nothing and yet
That doesn't make sense and
If you are going to die today don't marry
The love of your life—what does that leave them?
And the broken half-dozen Christmas cookies
In the wax paper signal Cupid's knock:
The headless snowman, the broken
Ornaments, the Christmas tree snapped
At the base. Jim, go on about what
You don't know, go on about it.
Hide what is in you elsewhere
So that what is in you stays safe.
Angel's Trumpet, admire the success
Of the plant, from Shiva's throat

To Jamestown delirium, to the yard
Full at the corner of Eleanor Dr.
And Connie Ave.—I don't want Bay
To touch the flower and yet how not to notice
The half-lily, half-insect purple mouth
Begging for attention. I spend less time
With Bay then I spent
With my older kids. Sadness lined like faux bois
Where arbitrariness keeps a child
Apart. The law required time and no other
Priority could insert an orange cone.
No delay re-routed the detour
Around the under construction.
Few don't enjoy Karan's Cashmere Mist
—expensive but you can't help but love
What that scent does to your cheeks,
Your eyes, its nipply ting. Let me ruin
Your relationship now, there are no exceptions,
One of you does not care about the car
They drive, the other does not care
About the destination. Is it okay if I log
Into your email? Is it okay if I hack
Your Facebook account?
Is it okay if I look at your text messages?
Well, of course it is, if I find what I am looking for.
I understand; let's talk; let's process;
This will not stop the cerumen dam
Layered as a defense against the tone
Of voice you once loved.
Love is the resistance to the wave,
To not swim away so far that the break

Can't be heard. Imagine a child, that child,
This child, Bay. Find the error in your seeing
And you find the error in your thinking.
Find the glass case for your reading glasses
And rename your cat Beatrice.
Your only hope? Never to never be found out.
Your only hope? When in undertow,
Swim parallel to shore. Rutger Hauer
Keeps showing up, he was there during your birth,
He was there in the first movie you watched
Together in high school, and he waits for you
On the TV in the garage: Monsieur Hawarden
To Blade Runner to Mata Hari.
The reason we whistle in the dark
Is the reason we whistle in the dark.
You hit the ace high straight on the turn
Making a pair of tens good.
The law of small numbers
Makes every flower an Angel's Trumpet—beautiful but deadly.
I'm not exactly sure how
To explain all of this to Bay.
How do I say, "You will be deceived,
I don't know anyone other than your parents
Who want what's best for you.
And even we will fail you. At least
I will." Are you still with me? No? Good.
On the counter, the roll of aluminum
Foil pulled halfway from the box
Aims like a small cannon at the fridge.
Whereas and whereas and whereas.
A tall glass of lemon water situates

A kind of yellow not far off in hue
From the beech Vejmon beneath,
And from this angle the far edge
Exits left and right are the lines
Visible in the glass. Dog toys litter
The couch, a spiky green ball
Like a cartoon sea creature rests
Between the far cushions,
The grey nylon chew toy
Peeks out from the back.
How long ago was it that we
Were skating on the meadow?
The three of us, wobbling, holding
Each other for support, the others
Skating circles around us.
Last night I saw Gillian at The Birthday Party,
When Nat yelled repeatedly, "The world is..."
I came to understand three quarters or less
Of anything suffices.
The broken guitar aims
And misses. Hide the soul everywhere:
In the cupboard, in the recipe for fish in a bag,
In the slices of fennel underneath the body, in the back
Of your colleague's desk drawer,
In the next book.
If lost, you don't have to look far or long.
Atop the lampshade, in the feel of the finial,
Leave some there.
In the caption to the photo of the backside
Of a stop sign reflecting triangles
Of twilight's geometry,

Leave some there.
Insert dream here. Insert civic history here.
Wave your hands in the web. Be prepared,
Scatter now; there will be no transitions.

Otters

Darkened ideas just out of reach over the kelp
Ceiling topped out at the surface of the currently
Calm ocean, where otters, directly in our line of sight,
Can't be seen. There is no way for me to reveal
What the chattering Steller's jay in the upper
Reaches of the eucalyptus had to say.
The almost straight lines of cormorants,
A windmill atop a steel transom like a splintered raven,
The bird of paradise behind a wall of stacked stone.
So please always be yourself, she said.
She said I can't be with you. She said, because
Of the others. Which yearns for the dimming
Cover to let slip the sky's dampening
Denials: dishonesty is the best policy.
Love the yarrow wound in the wrought iron.

Breaking Trail Improvisation XI

For when all things become lost
For when all things become a long walk
For forgetting
To find the lost memory of hummingbirds
To discover how time
With your permission
Cascades like dyspneic breaths meant to give the body protection
From the panic
Of misdirection
Leading to the sumptuousness of a brae in an open meadow
For eating nasturtiums
For lack of control
For the brain's self-identifying
Echo when it first sees Gomphaceae
And its geomorphic mirror
Of slot canyons over a rounded plain
For meadows and finches and shame
For the forgotten redness of the image spun in its yellowed, unreachable
    ether
Like a samsara tilting and spinning toward the sidewalk
For the worms and figs and overabundance of white turnips
For the days
For the horseflies, for the houseflies, for the spider lupine
For a hike to the hot spring
For the rubbings over the week of a forgotten dream remembered not in
    details but in the form of forgotten prayers hidden behind the veil of
    adolescence
For the air's poison
For the catamount resting on the slab aside the base of horsetail falls

For the spores from 1903, finding a limited conception of the possible
    and not settling
For the first tones of detrital slur slick in the air from decompiling all the
    constructs
Even that one, too
For the Polaroids
For the unopened
For the loam lifting its angels
For the spilled coffee in the wild rye.

Halfway

Walking the earth makes it clear our gods are overrated.
There is no order. Start at the end. Finish halfway through.
Walk the world with a watch that loses some time every few minutes
Prickly in the fingers, borage in the mouth is cucumber on the tongue.
The trail ends here. There is an order to finishing when through
The gap under the cone cupping the sun's arrival time in pink
Flowering, nasturtium on the tongue is radish in the mouth.
Being here, this is how it is. I can't control it. Nasturtium:
Naris 'nose' and torquere 'to twist'. The cone under the sap

Sunning the cup's arrival time in ink. Pigweed flickers like a green
Hairstreak under my uvula. Begin here. This is how it is. I can't
Control it. A Fairbanks Morse windmill, only the gears remain.
Pigweed flickers like a green hairstreak. Under my uvula
There is a cave I have lost myself in, devoured my sins
In a Fairbanks Morse open-gear windmill. What remains
But to walk the world with a watch that loses some time every few
Minutes. The cave that devoured my sins is in it, in that time
Walking the earth makes it clear our gods are overrated.

Full Stop

Picture the most pleasurable moment of your wildest dreams.
Go ahead. I'll wait.
You have become a thing concealed. A part of the kaleidoscope.
Between the field and the pasture is the meadow.
Unwind meadow, find mead. What is behind Isabelle?
Pixelate 1939 and read about fire, where hope collides with smoke.
Everything I have ever done will be forgotten, the speed of absence,
Of remembrance, is the half-life of the afterlife.
The etymology of death is the death of what you love.
Unwind the second person, unwind Isabelle, and find the meadow.
What is behind me?
A paper fir on a toothpick trunk stuck in a wine bottle cork.
Unwind, find Isabelle, and the insides of your worst memory.
A mason jar full of dried calendula in your mother's hand.
Cork the wine bottle and stick a toothpick in a paper box.
Build each birdcage with a full stop, each wire the stuff off
Of the cutting room floor. Go ahead. I'll wait. Unwind Isabelle.
Inside your worst memory, find me. The moth, gold and silvery black
Caught in the green net of the lace lichen. Build your cutting room floor
From the stuff of songbirds.
Between the field and the pasture is the meadow.
A picture of the most pleasurable moment of my wildest dreams.
The green net of lace lichen, the moth's body, the wings.
Dried calendula in a mother's hand, where hope collides with smoke.
Everything you have ever done will be remembered.

Firefly Nectar for Rebecca

Bluebottles in the finch's eye, tumbling in the dragonflies
Like an ashamed father. Shortly spinning time after time
The legs that insist on knees, like a song recalled word
For word and hung in the air while sleeping and dying.
Like an ashamed father, spinning time. After a time
One loves the blue of *Vermeer's Girl with a Pearl Earring*
For words hang in the air not while sleeping but dying
[Rebecca, I am thinking about you and our collage-making]
"Who can afford to enjoy a meadow?" Three times three.
One loves the hue of Vermeer's Girl with a Pearl Earring.
Write this line quickly to the prosody of the song's finch.
"Who can afford to enjoy a meadow?" Three times
I have delayed the bad news. How long, legs falter, I loop
And write this line quickly to the prosody of the finch's song.
The voice in her head asks, "Oh my god, am I loading the dishes
Again?" This is the bad news. Now, long legs falter, I loop
Rhythms, sasquatch, minotaur, snapdragons in a maze
Bluebottles in the finch's eye, tumbling in the dragonflies.

The Break Down

Two chambers, you see, one for the trimmings, one for the breakdown.
Building a compost bin requires an artful design.
I used 6 3x3 posts—one in each corner, two at the midpoint.
In the breakdown, let the work of worms compose the soil.
Building the compost bin requires a murderous design.
The end of last year's Rebellion thrived until uprooted
The worms do their work and break the compost down into dirt
Aside a jar of polar bear teeth, my mother's ashes.
Last year, Rebellion so recently undone, lasted a year
And I wonder, should I have let it continue to grow?
My mother's ashes? On a shelf, aside a jar of polar bear teeth.
An oil painting of her hangs somewhere. A girlfriend
The artist whose heart I broke
And I'm wondering, "Should I have let it all go?"
Despite this, I pulled the Rebellion out at the root.
Not long after after the oil painting, the artist whose heart I broke tried to
      hang herself
I yanked back the neck of the aging kale, the heart of the artichokes, and
      placed them in the bin.
I pulled the finished Rebellion out at the root.
I used six 3x3 posts. One in each corner two at the midpoint.
Like I said, it was me. I yanked their neck. I pulled out the heart.
I threw it all in the bin.
Two chambers, you see, one for the trimmings, one for the breakdown.

Otters II

A meadow forms, at high tide, a pebble
Catches between two rocks. My body
Is your body, I want to hurt you,
I want to hurt myself. Otters fly
Above the forest canopy. How do the dead
Negotiate? Mother, what red tape did Michelle
Cut to make it so? Smashed on the coastal
An intelligence released by bliss, an otter
Pulls paws under its chin, treads tail, dives.
Low-top chucks, socks stuffed, not quite
All the way in, charcoal from use, wet.
There is nothing quite like having just left
A wild meadow. Blue currents consider
The otter. Nothing is seen by all things.

Kindnesses

In Beardsley, the mask might represent
Giving liberty a kind of preference,
But this decadence was not meant
To burn the garden or the origins.
We are all criminals, bandits, the shape
Of our deeds permitted our state
Affairs: the poisoned bushtit, the net's
Free-tailed bat, a trash can, tin, shaken
Into the dump truck. At all times, I can't
Breathe. I assume I am ill. I assume you are ill.
Sometimes, I remember the spigot
Depends on something else.
The black spider's white dot, a dash
Of kindness, a kind of warning.

Hallucinations

The boulder on the ridgeline is not a condor.
The kelp on the surface is not a whale.
The truth laid bare is not a bear.

share   d

                time
         with ou   t

   weight

Let's Talk About Almost Dying After Stumbling Out of the Woods at 1 A.M. onto Highway 1 at Mile Marker 44 (Delta 22 & 28)

We light incense and we recover.
We as kilim or Greek key.
We as fiber or as knot or weave.
As round or square or other.
Discomfort has more intelligent
Things to say on the subject:
We as damask or circle link.
If I had a compass, I would get lost.
If I followed you to bed, I would already be there.
The plucked string of tinnitus
Rings in D-flat. The chameleon tongue
Within the cochlea. Blink and the scene
Changes. We laugh. We talk about
Almost dying while stumbling
Onto Hwy 101 at 1 a.m..
When the car hit me, I shit and puked
At the same time but otherwise,
I felt pretty good and headed on my way.
In "Dry Heat" by Cheekface
"Its laundry day anyway,"
Bay in yesterday's shorts and t-shirt.
Today at the slough, Bay described
What the minotaur looks like.
Nose ring, tinged with rust.
Wolfman arms. Goat legs. Bull horns,
Face, and nose...with a hammer,
The handle a red leather

With a series of silver rings
Presumably to better keep a grip.
If the function of narrative
Is but a psychological underpinning
Required to divide the blanket
Of the mystery from the disfigured self,
Then this compulsion.
And if the eye can only see
As the mind instructs
—I am aware that while staring
Right at you I will sometimes not see
Or hear you but be walking
Through a Nez Perce War Dance
Ceremony occurring circa 1900
—in fact, there is a picture of me there—
I am center of the frame, foreground,
Hands in my pockets, walking with head
down to the left. Pivot, head fake, shoot it.
No sign of the muskrat, until the swath at edge
Clawed with mud
Reveals where the grass ends through the steep
Edge to the water. The dog pushes the red ball
Underneath the couch where it cannot be reached.
Barks incessantly for a return.
The mind attends to the talk track
Even while the eyes try and follow the line.
Pain in the body has taken up residence
And does not pay rent.
Hope requires an oil change:
As if every line was peeled off the top
Of the prior. The perspective here pari passu.

If not given a job to do, the narcissist
Will indulge in self-diagnosis
And impale their body on your ache.
Insert as many misspellings as make sense.
Don't forget homonyms count.
Note on composition: why does the reader,
Or more specifically the expert, need politic
Inserted here—why the ask for acceptable
Humanism—when we know, we all know
Even the end of the world will not endure.
My mother sang me to sleep.
I sang my children to sleep,
Two songs all my children know,
"Three Little Birds"
And "Redemption Song."
Just because it is destructive
Does not mean it is not beautiful.
Perhaps because it is destructive it is beautiful.
The dead sing in some bones
And not in others. Today I drove
To San Jose to visit a catfish.
The empty space between the lines
Empties the space between the lines lining the space.
When out of olive oil, sear a piece of bacon
In a cast-iron skillet. Heat on high
Until fat renders the air with sow.
The grass seed from last year
Has taken hold around the rhetorical
Expression of feeling only the uninjured
Can express with such alignment.
Knee-deep fescue. The absence of constraints

Is the new constraint. Find where the light
Tilts and the slough goes glassy
And the sky settles across the surface
And the turtle's head, indistinguishable
From a stick, monitors our observation of the carp
Nosing into the detrital floor and insert
A list of active verbs -- the great blue heron
Coasts to a landing. As the feet touch the edge,
The 15 wild rabbits in the border field
Pause, the wind arrests, the wolf hound barking
In the distance halts, the boats
Idle in slow water, and no one
In the known world says a word. When
Everything in a standstill as a function
Of a completed circuit -- the frill
Of a Polaroid as an afterthought loses
Its moment -- a decade later
That same photo -- nearly discarded
— changes everything about you.
Every success story retells Dante
— because we can't have it any other way.
A family of quail rush about in search
Of a safety only the coyote solves.
In "Secret Plot" by Sonny & The Sunsets,
Oh its all so simple, "everything the world is doing to me."
The delta's cattails ripen as something
Like the middle of the year rushes
Towards us: a man running from a burning
Building. The plush brown flower
Head, smooth in the hand like the arm
Of a velvet jacket or the back of a short-haired tabby,

Signals to the heart to eat the eye.
I've decided to use cattails in my stir fry.
Linda has entered my writing studio
And flashes her tits at me, again.
This is when she is most prodigious
When I am focused on someone, or something, else.
At the base of the leaf shoot in the leaf blade,
The unobserved edible core.
Harvest them now, in a few weeks
No one will know the difference—
Let's ignore Bay walking next to me,
Next to you, for no good reason other than
Nothing has taken him from us
—and my unearned expectation that no one could.
Let's ignore lizard season, the frame of the door,
The mailbox, the gate post, the stones
Holding the shape of the earth,
The car window, the rubber boot, the backpack—
The network of the brain structures
Where the mind goes to wander.
A pregnant woman
Holds the whole system together
And I'm sure when I tell you
The stewardess I got pregnant
With Bay's new brother is moving in
Will delight you.
And the injury inflicted defines the depth of ownership
—and only long after exiting
The embrace of a consciousness
Does a consciousness know the observed,
Not being or thinking,

Have you had enough of me yet? I have
And if you have listened this long just know
You are likely only one of a handful.
The Cal Poly student with the Greek
Word "poiima" tattooed on her arm
(or was it the Hawaiian word "poina"—I forget)
Behind the counter at Surfside Donuts in Pismo Beach
Has changed her major from Bible Studies to Nursing.
Lit afterthoughts snake charcoal into carbon.
The smoke of a plum-colored
Bomb hides the fuse burned to the nib.
Flitters dance within jumping jacks.
Parachutes and pistils—
Peonies and palm trees—these ideas confetti the landscape.
Up above and below...
In "Till the End of the Day" the last studio recording
Chilton ever made—the lyrics express the simplest truth
"You and me we're free, we do as we please,
From morning 'til the end of the day."
Today's allegory: Lent's charcoal cross
Smudges the third eye. Pause. Please leave.
Go watch the series of films you imagine I just deleted.
For your convenience
I have set up three viewing stations
At 199 Taber Pl in San Francisco.
Bay licks the yellow lemon-flavored lollipop
With the scorpion inside.
The arthropod suspended in the translucence
Holds the arc of the stinging telson,
Of threat in a comic vanished spring of light,
Like the demands of doubt

That take on any desire—every wave function
Describes murmuration
And one must commit, and commit fully,
To not stop seeing the ant colony
Optimization as one of many but not the only way
The community can solve the problem.
Consider the Monte Carlo algorithm
—if you want the best possible solution when you
Have too much to consider—try including
The most random answer possible. What
The algorithm shows?
Every light on at 12:42 a.m. between 3rd street and 4th street
On May 11th in 2016 caused one pupil to dilate.
"Why kill any giraffe, let alone a black giraffe?" asks Bay.
The emphasis of his cheekbones a parentheses
Around the rhetorical expression of feeling
Only the uninjured can express with such alignment.
He sees my lack of reaction as a kind of implied dampening of his awe.
My immunity to the horrors of the everyday
Has transplanted in him a lowering of expectation of others
That can't be weeded out.
People will kill, animals, each other, ideas, themselves—
Damaging others is what we do. I say to him,
"Remember when we were at the Barry McGee
Show and we were laughing at the mix
Of graphic arts and found objects?
You made fun of me because I sat on the couch
In the Fong Health Center
And got paint on the seat of my pants?"
He said, "Yes, yes I do."
The universe hangs around your neck.

The tin locket with an imprint of a belladonna,
The leaf on the front opens to three words.
The punk lit in the first line has ashed down
To the last few seconds of the stick's ember.
We dance in the wake of the tourbillon,
We ache in the falling strobes,
We submerge the self in the jellyfish,
And we arrive at the magic carpet.
I am a spiral. You hold me fast
When I would otherwise wander.
You willow. We pattern
When the vanished garden forgets the memory.

Meditation IX

You were supposed to be connecting my bald spot
To my third eye, my left; the right side to my
Breath. I killed three horseflies instead.
The first found my ear after a handful of flybys.
Landed on the lobe of my left ear, scuttled
Counterclockwise from 12 to 3. I'm sure, breathe,
It was about to bite me. Let the...I grazed
My hand through the air as a warning. And relax.
Shooed, I felt pacified. And out. That fly returned.
And transition. Release. Got'em! Something about
Listen to the eaves—something about time your breath.
The second horsefly landed on my forearm, nested
In my arm hair. I could see it crouching to take
A dump. And one. The opposite hand moving like a giant
Bird. Take the shape most comfortable to you. Dead.
Flat on my back on the swelling earth, the third lands
On my lips. I'm ready. Lips, pursed, a quick deep breath.
Thup.

Nightbreeze with Dark Olive Tint

The witch's teeth pock the bedside
And the elongated applause of the last
Set of residual radio waves vanish.

Everyone will never know; everyone knew
Better what this constellation next door
Could do for you. Linda, beautiful

In Spain. Mix the composite, breath
Without disease. As the set, it flattens
Into an orange-pink, blued-yellow pagoda

Of near enough. Can't anyone see you?
Latch the door, keep the tired earning
Their keep. Sleep, disorder your madness

While fire season burns across the state
Of things. As a child, in the barn, my friends
Lit the frayed end of a coil of rope on fire

Down here at the end of love, who reads
The cards? Long after, at the end of all
Things, a blue-bead lily where ash once was.

Lemma Variation XVII

No shape is better than any other.
The depth of the wound determines how
Long it will take to heal. First things
First. How many tattoos do you have?
Don't listen to the waves of the ocean
Or the chirping of the frogs. Firebrand
The cheek, pierce the nose. Obedience's
Demands in a normal grazing season,
Horses will favor this. When was the last
Time you came upon red larkspur? And
What were you thinking when you did?
A lack of control over what is happening
To you will exaggerate the disaffections.
The awnless lemma, spikelets asking
Please do not stay if you can't abide,
But if you can, obey, enjoy, play the part.

Loadout

The Pa'alante pack ways in at glances,
Stuff sleeping bad into the bottom—no lack,
Shove tent rolled around stakes—push
Until slugs. Cinch sack, brighter, clove, iso,
Cup-kitchen. Compress puff into its own socket.
Layer bag of instant coffee, a handful of crags
Of ready-mad beans. Noodles, brains into a dyneema
Sack—roll top tight. Sardine kitchen, denied goods,
And jacks perpendicular to lent. Layer three—complete.
Tightly wound in a see-through: chlorine tabs, high-grade
Water tilter—loveliness the size of a toll of lifesavers.
Two empty bladders folded tall, flyweight
When empty. A water gobble, goose items: first laid,
Rope, sunglasses, nightcap. Fast actions: harpen the knife.
And to take sure we play lost, do regret the map.

Like Frost on the Wings of a Last Autumn Monarch

As a comet

Like a disco ball

Like a moth drawn to a lighthouse's deception

Like a moon behind clouds howling at oblivion

Like a mirage

As laughter

As threads of moonlight woven into the most pleasant of nightmares

Like the pier's piling just below the surface of low tide

Like consequences drifting in a sea of icebergs

Like a meadow

Like a peacock in Central Park

Like a surfer in storm break

As a firecracker exploding in super slo-mo

Like a blank wall emerging from the mural

A Transect Study of Shooting Stars

The bumblebee bypasses the Ohia Tree. Mandalas
Hang fractalized space in the empty spaces between branches.
In the throat, [put both your hands on your throat,

I'll wait] the yellow burst from within the purple tepals
Of blue-eyed grass. [Squeeze.] Observe:
A love from those who love you seduces the desired.

Housekeeping walked in on a guest shooting stars.
Trunks of trees smoothed and pitched against the chest
Edgings rubbed over and over with the dice roll

Of the moon's pull. Pick up a handful of soil:
[I'll wait.] rendzina, alluvial, peaty or loamy, the cryo
The fluv, or the clay: taste it, dead catch in the throat.

Test Survey Beta

I can't make out the line 'tween fire's flare, And the osprey's soaring. Can't discern where a spill kit ends and where the day's last light blends with Miner's lettuce, at the center the milkmaid's baize. Cold-soaked oats mix with goat camp's sky.

Madonna and Mary Magdalene hum like mosquitoes like poison oak lining our secret heaven.

I can't fathom it, can't reckon the distinctions of fire's beacon and the osprey's shadow. Can't untangle the twine of a spill kit, from the sun's descent. Miner's lettuce embraces a meadow of milkmaid as cold-soaked oats blur into goat camp's list. You and me and Mary, it's tangled, we're a blur.

We dance to elude whispered secrets of damselflies. Words left unsaid: the clamor of demand. Mosquitoes hum in evening's quiet demands; what rolls in poison oak.

I find myself lost, you know?

A labyrinth where fire blurs with an osprey's shadow. In the twilight, I'm unsure whether it's a spill kit or the sun bidding "adieu." Miner's lettuce and milkmaids merge. a reverie of cold-soaked oats and the sulky essence of goat camp.

You, me, and Mary, the boundaries fade, like those between the persistent hum of mosquitoes and unyielding desire.

The tangled brambles of blackberry, and poison oak: lies. A secret sanctuary, a glimpse of heaven.

House wren, the hole dweller, we reside within, we croon of, sulphury hot springs, forsaken bridges, phantom vessels. We hunger for the delicate flutter moths and monarchs, for the industrious chitter of ants and wasps, for the nocturnal serenade of crickets, and the dayspring of grasshoppers. Our nests they're woven from Spanish moss, opossum fur, zucchini blossoms, and the lingering aroma of patchouli.

I cant. I can't. I can't resist the siren call. Foreverness beckons. Take in the robin egg. I can't say that love never wanes. I can't draw breath. Don't abandon us. What does it mean to forsake? Its lines like tremens off basalt. It runs away from me before I can inhale, I can't catch it. Can't declare that love will never falter. The tape measure rests beside the cache of business cards. But I must confess, I can't halt my wanderings, the ceaselessness, I won't beg. I can't make you stay, but there's something you must know: I can't stop, please don't let me go. I can't make you stay, I am unkind, and I can't resist the allure of wildflowers ever beckoning in Moon Meadow. Linger with me.

Aerial

If wilderness can be sung
You can voyage and be seen.
When you can no further.
The runner's fruit, a lambent
Stand of poison oak aglow
With Astrid's trifold response.
The unmaintained trail here
Loses somewhere. Gods despise
Himalayan blackberry
Choking out California
You can be heard by the sung,
If the seen can be wildness.
Tin cloth sleeves zip through canes
Under a curved orrery
That asks nothing of us but
What void, what trail, what dusk?
Again matters nonetheless –
All the matted self-destruction,
The unmaintained analogue
Surrounds us and avoids us.
Is listlessness erotic?
Across the ligature, ropes
Bound. Even the air is ill.
Unhatched turtles in a nest
Aside the Brewer's blackbirds
Unfed going on two days.
If the sung can be wildness
Then the heard can be seen by you.

Passarelas Meant to be Read While Listening to Bob Dylan's "One More Cup of Coffee"

Like every line after the turn
Like the heads of wild turkeys in tall grass
Like insomnia's promise: no harm will come to you while I am here
Like begging for disrespect

We heard a crow right here gluck the sound of an unlatched gate
We need a car horn in the distance over there [identify where I'll wait]
A hybrid nature challenges a precise definition.

Like phenomenological trust fall exercises
Like air the color of worn leather
Like panic

Like thirst's angrier second second cousin
Like everything, this is just an exercise
We need a canopy of stars over the Santa Lucia in here.

[I'll wait]. We need a hound shaking itself dry.

A Poem Called "Wasteland" Meant to be Read While Listening to "Traveling Riverside Blues"

The meadow's troublesome sedge
Dreams of burning to the ground.

Melville's little similes a few pages from here.
Wild boar in the arroyo, piglets index

The dust of memory, a spider's web
Of ash, an FYI from the Kilkare fire.

The lick observed the moon's nonetheless:
I don't believe in love, I don't believe in love.

Was it 1907 when we soaked the skin
Out of our bones at Mendenhall Springs?

Snouts root in the tomato garden.
The throat of the gods is sore. The dust

Is ash and Meleager failed to appease
Us again. That green spray is not a weed

Rather, Ithuriel's spear. Unbloomed. You
Cannot remove a harpoon from a heart.

Susurration on Loop

As if surplus gravity netted the surface of my skin
And pulled. Like the sound of a door opening then slamming shut.
Like a coyote running ahead of you on the trail

To catch the quail you are about to spook.
A hawk glide mimics a heartbeat, gives permission,
A river known by its susurration alone.

We know the black bear is just ahead because of its spoor.
We poke the manzanita berry and the wild cherry
In the scat, say, "I guess that answers that question."

Swallows unstring the gnats pixelating the wi-fi.
Wildflowers, sedges, grasses, no one, no one.
Even the air is ill. What void? What dusk?

I dreamt my veins a sort of trail map
To unexplored territories with unpredictable weather.

Dispatch from Sundown Gone Sideways

My hands are in the sink, and the dog
Suns in hands of the backyard's daydream.
Who can't adore the tangled root
Of the boots at the foot of the door? All the vernal
Water drips off the table to the floor
of the room. The Ohlone's trail is every trail.
A rise removes weight from your back,
The longer it runs. Monkeyflower,
A misnomer of misnomers in a world of misnomers
Purpled and pinked to the hummingbird's delight.
I have come in the back door of your house,
Wait for prologue at high tide, and watch
It drown out the very song you hope to sing.
Someone give this active skin a honeycomb. A sheen
Flashes from within like sudden starlings.

The Ester of Whitethorn and Wild Quinine Gratitudes

Wild oat's envy and yellow rocket's secret lover.
This trailhead, leaning over, welcomes others.
Tarantulas cross the road like childhood
Dreams, how many years will it take to sound
Like someone else. "Save poor Bob if you please."
Frictions in the process only visible
In the spectre of decomposition. Benicio
Del Toro, like an earwig, will not depart, and I'm
Wearing him like a cloak. Never before have we
Been so aware of how the world touches us, our hands
Grazing the edge of a door handle, breath sidling
Along the ear of another, our love bends, no, arcs
Towards and away from forever and never. Nothing
Lasts forever nothing last forever nothings last forever.

Sur

Detrital mud gives up its air as I fill my dirty water bladder.
By pinning Black's King Knight, White threatens NxP.
Deer knee-deep at the far edge. Coyote scat at my feet. Imagine
Reaching up to scoop a cup full of that sky. Thirst.
How many hours will pass before I find the next chance
To drink some water? The rock fringe, brutal in its angst,
Impervious to my need, vibrates as a breeze strolls by. Shaped
Like sex, what call of what bird is that? Your songbirds
Circle, never far from my daydreams. Nested in nearby fir.
Noisy in the lovegrass. "Am I really going to drink this?"
Warm and swampy, almost salty, and a hint of mint:
At first, my tongue resists.

74

naked

views

between

cottonwoods

On the Drive to School a Coyote Crossed the Road Again Again

Strawberries contain as much water as watermelon.

The well-ordered fields keep April open until May,

The lapse reminding the hand of a grandmother
Pouring heavy cream into a glass bowl.

The whisk next to the tumbler of whiskey,
At the time who new Manhattan was a place?

A beheaded strawberry wobbles off the edge
Of the wooden cutting board.

Does understanding a reasonable life require
A criminal mind?

Her Tinder date tried to feed her right-hand
To the kitchen's garbage disposal. So I was an upgrade.

When questions end the lilac's conversation,
No zookeeper's daughter will defend the observations.

On the drive to school, the conversation turns to Zeno's Paradox
And degrades into fascinations of Algebra:

If John leaves New York at 9 am traveling 60 miles
An hour and Amanda leaves Pittsburgh

At 10 a.m. traveling 80 miles an hour
—371 miles according to Google Maps, Where?

How can you tell? Can you change the voice in your head?
Will they meet? Who asked, "have you tried incomplete sentences?"

The voice in your head is not your voice.
A body contains more bacterial cells than human cells.

Turtles swim in the legs of the water table. Crawdads in the joints.
Salmon in the dowels. Stripers in the grain.

No departure obscures daydreams
With schoolhouse red better than the passenger

You left behind, feet dangling out the window,
"Cuz i'm the doo hop skotcher"

Like the Stoop Kids riff in "Padiddle."
Hours later, the green-leafed tops still green

The air with dirt's glib afterthoughts,
The back of a throat's reflex to the spoiled fruit's endlessness

Denies the self-denying owners of uncoded codes.
The wig of the body hides the joy

When we don't disguise decadence or confuse depravity
With pleasure. The next hidden bias? Anything more than hues.

On the drive to school a coyote crossed the road again again.
Bay said, "Again?"

This means at certain angles we can't be sure about love:
A boy drowning in his own cigarette smoke

In an apartment with the pull-down as a front door.
A lover has replaced the stars

With her own wishes for what others want to steal.
Now remains apart from then.

The dream? To want what others want to have.
The sun, full of tomatoes, over-ripens in the neighbor's garden.

In the seventh row of the third field, they meet,
Their sons notice each other and exchange a nod.

Yes, them. Like Danny says in Gates of *Gates of Heaven*,
"A broken heart is something that everyone should experience."

But let's not talk about talking about that.
My kiss on Bay's forehead,
Like an early-summer strawberry, reddish, bittersweet, and 90% water.

Cosmorama: The B-side of the EP

Mouse barley too near the isobutane
Stove, the green of my tent near yours,
Civic twilight stretches into the conversations.

Shakespeare, if we weren't talking Shakespeare,
We wanted to: Smith Meadow feeling
Like something intentionally hidden –

Omitted from Prospero's maps. On stage
How to light a place unknown
To both actors and audience? The frail

Cub halfway up the burnt stalk of a pine
Sniffed the wind in search of our camp's
Tuna casserole. My sleeping bag napped

On my sleeping pad. Socks and shoes aired
Just outside the door. All the wildness
Does not care about you, or me, or any of this

Bluestem or foxglove or side oat.

Reversing Creamery Meadow's Daydream

Before we named the western fescue, always
The Ohlone. Before Rick James's "Super Freak"
Always the black oaks. Before the palatable forbs
Always subformations. Pick up the fall line.

Before the Instagram posts fencing the streambed
Always the xero-pulse of the iotic meadow.
Before the removal of the splinter
Always restore the root vegetables.

Of the 126 possible meadows, according to theory,
Only 32 have been identified in the field.
We've dreamt more ways to meadow than we have found:
Moist, wet, serpentine, transitional, perpetual.

Of this, we can be certain the meadow we have found
Ourselves in, thankfully, does not exist. Notice
The diminutive elephant heads, the alpine flames
The contour map of the bodies, all twelve of them.

Backcountry Biopic, Somewhere Past Sykes Hot Springs on a Closed Section of the Pine Ridge Trail

Alone, this far from you, everyone
I'm bushwacking from what was once
Apple Tree Camp to Mt. Diablo, biblical
I know. I forgot to tell you
How I fell a few feet off a scramble
Into the creek and knocked myself out.
I will forget to tell you after sleeping
Alone between two trees for a few nights
How tendinitis all but stopped me
From taking a few steps a minute.
I forgot to tell you about cutting
My way through a 40-yard stand of poison
Oak. But I will not forget to tell you
How I stood at the summit and watched
26 and 42, two condors, soar below me.

Meadow Shade Made of Body Parts

Meadows do not have deep water tables
And sometimes originate from bodies of water.
Split me open, I was here with you then.

A lime-rich lake, a weedy pond, human appetites:
Livestock, fodder, water, pasture, play.
Is this trail where I left my last snakeskin?

They live as a part of and apart from these woods:
Meadows do not run off. Meadows margin. Meadows
Slender. Sky parlor's immense second cousin

Architected to fear the lodgepole pine. Love
The lodgepole pine. Purposeless, they live forever
As the shape of what can be imagined and present

Sensory impressions of "completeness" and complete
"Interconnection"; uniform material nowness
[A Polaroid: nape, trunk, calf, the turned head's chin]

Yet structured like the Copernican graph of a flower:
Bract into sepals into petals, stamen into pistil.
The knee of the Little Sur turns in the underbelly of my skin.

The stem of the meadow the conceptualization
Of the medulla oblongata: as meadow is meadow.
Can light dislike its wave? There is a ghost within.

Black Sage and the Blessings of the Penultimate

Linda, I am far away from you now. Far from
The place we first found something other,
Some world hidden in each other, far from
Our Catholic high school, something maybe
In the birches. No shape is any better
Than any other. My last hike to the vernal
Fall, showing up as it does during melt,
How many other times of the year might I have
Walked right past this spot. Here in the sun,
When I lay naked in the light. I realize
There are few places left where I can lay
Naked in the light. This, here, is one of them.
Injustices overshadow us. The cypress looms.
We are in the space between noticing
The cormorant, the shadow toll of the waves
And the lemure of what the wind shakes
Across the floor of the pool. What's sound?
Who can resist the red maids, the star tulips,
The black sage and here, in my hand, hemlock.

The Gnarl in the Maple Fallen Across Grindstone Creek

I have not overheard enough to get started
Yet, promises, promises. Pico Blanco started
All things. Double down, evening rhythms
Settle in. She said, "Always eat your best
Meal first." After more miles than I count
I spoon the beans and songbirds into my mouth.
$\frac{3}{4}$ & $\frac{6}{8}$ signatures of cliffside down drafts
And rice and seabirds. A harbor seal
Among the rocks castling the whitewash.
Will you come with me to the meadow of youth?
A forgotten church leaning on the hill,
Abandoned churches feel more filled
With the possible than the maintained.
Missouri sun stretches the creek bed with a shadow
After a day of walking toward source
I am not a boy anymore I am all these broken
Devices: a compass, our bias, the voice of god.

Cithaeron Shares a Meal with His Mistress

Each lure in the water dressed in dyed feathers,
Beardsley perfumed his wooden roses.
The snake drinks from the shape of the stream.
My feet sort sand between your toes.
What comes in the night? The love letter
You sent, I will never respond to. The tape
Unwinds, and the binding of the book undone.
I am the god of mountains, the god of deceit.
Unwound along the edge of the switchbacks
Reveal you, dancing, ahead of me on the trail
And no looking back. Your water will run
Dry, and the memory of me will pass by
And not offer any relief; a cave's damp
Light does not discern. Rejecting a fury
Differs from bad weather in only the wind's
Direction. Lick the brackish remains of our
Smoked mullet from my bluing fingers.

[Insert Title Here]

A hand moves across the table like a giant bird.
While fucking me, your hand snatched a horsefly from the periphery.
Am I somebody who hurts people? I am somebody who hurts people.
The table moves under my hand like a giant bird.
What do we call the empty space between winter's branches?
Exhausted, I can walk no further, and I take the next step.
Like everything, this is just an exercise:
I'm typing this on a Corona Standard, in the age of Corona,
While you drink a Corona, and applaud the sunset's corona.
24 one-inch squares punched from trail maps, wilderness guides, and
    wallpaper samples
Reassembled to resemble one's interior designs.
I am somebody people hurt. Hiding between the lines
Are all of your songbirds?
Two pelicans skim the ocean surface.

[Insert Title Here II]

Like a walking stick
We have more choices than we think we have
The flower of the water lemon pleases more than its passionate fruit.
Is that true?
Monarchs on the cover, monarchs caught in the web of the spider
Lupine, like a meadow,
Like a walking stick.
What choice did I have? It was me.
The tansy says I have done what you likely think I have done.
In the dusk the Venn diagram of yellows.
The fool's tarot card on the edge of a knife,
The ChatGPT of hummingbird beaks in the snapdragons
Like a meadow,
Like a walking stick.
The guitar without measures razed the wild rye.

Untitled

Beneath the loam, loam-like gate.

Inside the clay bowl, bowl-shaped hands.

Around the silt, the shadows of glaciers.

Above white-throated swift, prayers to the tree of heaven.

Within the song of the dark-eyed junco, an unwritten thesis.

Ever present patchouli, the suffering distances of seals at bay.

Look long enough, and you see condors in the distance.

Look long enough, and you see everything except wood slat fences,

Which is the same thing as seeing only rock salt in a wooden spoon.

Because Funk #49 by the James Gang is impossible not to love.

Because the voicemail from a granddaughter wishing her grandpa happy
    birthday is impossible not to love.

Because the experiences we substitute for honey are impossible to not
    love.

The shibari's cross hitch between fingers and wrists

Lists the room, and the ladder to the loft loses its balance.

As a Desolate Peak Drifting Over a Cloud

As a god

Like a wasteland warmed by the untouched fires of ordinary men

Like lightning seizing the night

Like the unfulfilled glow of midnight sky as distant and unreachable as an idea's shadow

Like a shadow near dusk

Like a creation shattered into a thousand mirrors

Like its own creation

Like unspoken ships in a box of ice

Like a thief climbing a crumbling wall

Like a weeping child

As fog over a moor

Like a once great castle haunting the memory of a villain's ghost

Like a foal

Like a blotted canvas

Acknowledgments:

a chapbook, "intervals of," with Rebecca Resinski, an erasure of Sir Arthur Conan Doyle's *Sign of the Four*, Blue Bag Press

2 Couplets from a collaboration with Rebecca Resinksi, an erasure of Sir Arthur Conan Doyle's *Sign of the Four,* ""Couplet 11-14" and "Couplet 82-47," Eleven and a Half Magazine

2 Quartets from a collaboration with Rebecca Resinski, an erasure of Sir Arthur Conan Doyle's *Sign of the Four,* "Quartet 27 - 53 - 73 - 132" and "Quartet 80 - 121 - 9 - 118," The Tiny

"5 Quartets" from a collaboration with Rebecca Resinski, an Erasure of Sir Arthur Conan Doyle's *Sign of the Four*, Queen Mobs Teahouse

"Delta 22: We Laugh. We Talk about Almost Dying While Stumbling onto Highway 101 at 1 A.M." Basalt

"Delta 23: A Spider Web Across the Trail the Morning after a Night of Rain," Pif Magazine

"Delta 26: On the Drive to School a Coyote Crossed the Road Again Again," Goat's Milk

"Firefly Nectar for Rebecca" and "Working Backwards," Subtropics

"Meadow Shade Made of Body Parts," Antiphony

"Halfway" & "Full Stop," Weber – The Contemporary West

David Koehn won the May Sarton Poetry Prize with his first full-length manuscript, "Twine" (Bauhan Publishing, 2013). He released a collection analyzing Donald Justice's approach to prosody titled *Compendium* (Omnidawn Publishing, 2017). Omnidawn Publishing also brought out his second full-length collection, *Scatterplot*, in 2020. Koehn has a forthcoming chapbook, "intervals of," from a collaboration with Rebecca Resinski, which Blue Bag Press is set to publish. Koehn's writing has appeared in several chapbooks and across a wide range of literary magazines including distinguished publications such as *Kenyon Review*, *New England Review*, *Alaska Quarterly Review*, *Rhino*, *Volt*, *Carolina Quarterly*, *Diagram*, *McSweeney's*, *The Greensboro Review*, *North American Review*, *The Rumpus*, *Smartish Pace*, *Hotel Amerika*, *Gargoyle*, *Zyzzyva*, and *Prairie Schooner*. He earned his BA in Creative Writing at Carnegie Mellon and an MFA in Creative Writing at the University of Florida.

SUR
by David Koehn

Cover design by Jeffrey Pethybridge
Cover typeface:
Interior design by Laura Joakimson
Interior typefaces: Didot and Dapifer

Printed in the United States
by Books International, Dulles, Virginia
Acid Free Archival Quality Recycled Paper

Publication of this book was made possible in part by gifts from
Katherine & John Gravendyk in honor of Hillary Gravendyk,
Francesca Bell, Mary Mackey, and The New Place Fund

Omnidawn Publishing Oakland, California
Staff and Volunteers, Spring 2024
Rusty Morrison & Laura Joakimson, co-publishers
Rob Hendricks, poetry & fiction editor,
& post-pub marketing
Jeffrey Kingman, copy editor
Sharon Zetter, poetry editor & book designer
Anthony Cody, poetry editor
Liza Flum, poetry editor
Kimberly Reyes, poetry editor
Elizabeth Aeschliman, fiction & poetry editor
Jennifer Metsker, marketing assistant
Rayna Carey, marketing assistant
Kailey Garcia, marketing assistant
Katie Tomzynski, marketing assistant
Sophia Carr, production editor